Here For Now

2009

Stephanie Jacobson

Printed in the United States of America.

CONTENTS

CONTENTS
(CON'T)

CONTENTS
(CON'T)

got your number

Everyone knows what you're doing here
What your plan is
No matter how much you try to
Play innocent
They've got your number
So what else can you do
But give them exactly
What they expect?

free fall

Somewhere along the way
Things went horribly wrong
And it was all over before
You even knew it had begun
Now you're left
Spiraling out of control
In some dizzying free fall
That you have no idea
How to stop

less than stellar

Look,
I don't know what you people expect
From me
But I can't be everything
To everyone
I've tried
And the results have been
Less than stellar

try holding on

I feel like we've lost touch
Somewhere along the way
The only reason it's not over
Is because we just haven't let go
It's an out of sight
Out of mind
Type of thing
But all it takes is a smile
And ten minutes of
Conversation
To make me think maybe
We should try holding on
Just a bit longer

not enough time

I have way too much to do
And not enough time
To get it all done
Somewhere along the way
I'm letting someone down
Because whatever I decide
To sacrifice
In order to get to
Everything else
Is gonna be the one thing someone else
Is looking forward to

back-handed

I think all compliments
Should be given
In a back-handed way
Keeps things more
Interesting
That way

not good enough

My word is not good enough
To be taken
And my opinions only matter
To me
So I keep to myself
And smile like some idiot
When engaged in conversation

no need for words

Laying in your bed
Your hands trailing a lazy path
Along my back
Down my leg
I smile
And snuggle up closer
Nuzzle at your neck
There's no need for words
It's not long before
Our breathing settles into a
Synchronized rhythm
Signaling sleep is soon
I tilt my head ever so slightly
Allowing me to place a soft kiss
To your cheek as you
Pull me closer
Our bodies intertwined
My frame fitting against yours
Like this is where I'm meant to be
This is where I belong

to be said

There's something to be said
About holding on to your feelings
Keeping them to yourself
Sure it breeds resentment at times
But at least you're not burdening
Others with your shit

change

It's funny how quickly one's opinion
Can change
About something they used to enjoy
When made to feel guilty
About it
For whatever reason
The guilt was brought on

come back around

I want to go back
To the way things used to be
Not all that long ago
When we used to
Be able to talk
To share in similar interests
But you don't have the time
Or desire
To do so anymore
So I'll just wait
On the sidelines
And hope someday soon
You'll come back around

out of my system

I need to get my head straight
Find someone I can talk to
Someone who will listen
And not judge
Someone who will just let me say
Whatever I need to say
Until it's all
Out of my system
And who will hold their tongue
With the advice
Until I ask for it

spectrum

I'm the most self-centered
Yet
Self-loathing person
I think I know
And I'm not sure
How you can be at two such ends
Of the spectrum
At the same time
But I am

of you

I wake up in the morning
Curled around my pillow
With a smile on my face
Because my first thoughts
As I awake
Are of you

too personally again

I'm taking things
too personally again
which means I'm in
this constant state
of hurt and sad
when I should be looking at
things in the opposite light
it makes me want to
close myself off from
everyone
and every thing
and wallow
but I know that never works out well
so I'm trying to be upbeat
optimistic
while at the same time
I'm waiting for the next shoe to drop

boost my ego

You're such a boost to my ego
Which is something I totally need
You make me remember
I'm still the girl
I used to be
You make me feel
Beautiful and sexy
And that's something
I like feeling

nothing more

I can't believe
I'm actually contemplating
Meeting up with you
For the night
In a far away city
But I am
Just thinking about
How wonderful it would be
To spend the night
Curled up next to you
Naked
And spent
From a passion filled night
Just the thought
Makes me want to
Figure out a way
To make this little fantasy
Come true
But as nice as it sounds
I know it's nothing more
Than a dream

right place, right time

You make it easy
This whole idea
Of moving on with my life
It was one of those
Right place
Right time things
A subtle touch
A warm smile
A sparkle in your eyes
And I was hooked

Sometimes I wonder
If we're moving too fast
That maybe this won't be
A forever thing
But then you go and do something
Ridiculously sweet
And totally unexpected
And I remember how much
I'm falling in love with you

content

I love that you're so content
With just curling up in bed
At night
Sharing a few kisses
Before settling in
With me
Against your chest
Your strong arms wrapped around me
Keeping me close
Keeping me safe

one more poem

This poetry thing
Is a tricky thing
At times it feels
Like I've said
All I have to say
And I'm just repeating
Myself
At other times
This fresh idea
Springs onto the page
Giving me hope
That there's
One more poem
Left in me

thinking about you

I find myself
Thinking about you
At the strangest times
In line at the bank
Driving to the store
Waiting in traffic

push over

The longer I keep my feelings inside
The harder they are to control
For once I'd like to
Get it all off my chest
And let people know how
Pissed off I am
And how I'm tired of being
The fucking push over
But
I won't
I'll keep it to myself
Let it simmer
Boil under the surface
Like I always do

i wonder if...

I wonder if
You're free this weekend
To get together
And have a little fun

I wonder if
I asked you
Whether or not you'd
Tell the truth

I wonder if
Those sweet things
You've been saying to me
Are genuine and real

I wonder if
We'd met at a different time
And a different place
If this could be
Something real

three o'clock

It's three o'clock in the morning
I'm lying here in my bed
Pen and paper in hand
Trying to sort out my thoughts
And turn them into something useful
But my mind keeps drifting
To thoughts of you
Wondering what you're doing
At three o'clock in the morning
Wherever you are

all it takes

Just a simple hello
And I melt
That's all it takes
A few more words
Nothing special
Nothing fancy
And I'm done for

can't win

It's late
In the evening
And I should be asleep
But I'm not
Because there's
Work to be done
Trying to meet a deadline
I'm too far behind on
But
I suppose you can't win
If you don't even try,
Right?

the heat

The heat outside
Can't begin to rival
The heat between us
As you stare at me
From across the room
And I smile

seems so right

It seems so soon
But it seems so right
You slipping that ring
Onto my finger
No big scene
No grand gesture
Just softly and sweetly

no need

Lying in bed
Window open
Light breeze blowing through
Curled against you
Your hand lightly dancing
Along my back
As I draw lazy circles on
Your chest
With my fingertips
No need for words
No need for touches to
Become more than they are
Just being
In the moment

seemed to click

I'm still amazed
By you
By us
Even though we haven't
Been together that long
And we're still learning
Each other's
Ins and outs
Ups and downs
Yet,
In some ways
It feels like we've known
Each other
For so many years
Maybe we were friends
Or lovers
In some long ago past life?
Whatever the reason
We just seemed to click
From the first hello
And we haven't looked back since

something to do

I've been up and down that highway
So many goddamn times
In the past few weeks
That the idea of going
Somewhere
Has lost it's appeal
But tomorrow
I'll be off again
Climbing in the car and
Heading down the road
Blame it on where I live
And the fact
There's fuck all to do
Around here
So I'm left with no choice
But to travel down the road
To another town
Another place
Just to find something to do
For the afternoon

think of me

I wonder if you think of me
When I'm not around
And if you do think of me
What it is you're thinking
I wonder if you're really
As into me as you say you are
If you really think I'm sexy
Or if those are just words
To get me into bed

the memory of

I still can't get the memory of
How good you smell
How good you kiss
How good you make me feel
Out of my head
And I'm not sure
Those are memories
I want to forget

deadlines be damned

Two-thousand words down
Eight-thousand to go
And only four more days
To do it in

Fifty-one pages down
Forty-nine pages to go
And only four days
To do it in

If it wasn't for the fact
I've barely been home
For the past three weeks
I wouldn't be this far behind

But
I was off having fun
And living life
And there are
Certain opportunities
That don't come along
All that often
So you've gotta take them
as they come
Deadlines be damned

running out

I'm running out of time
And
Running out of ideas
But I'm not ready to give up
Quite yet
Figure I might as well
Make the most of
What little time
And what few ideas
I have left
And see how much
I can get done

solitary bliss

He wakes in the morning
Before she does
Just to watch her sleep
Hair splayed on her pillow
As the morning sun
Dances through the window
And across her face
She's like an angel to him
In these precious early moments
With the gentlest of touches
He strokes her cheek
And she instinctively smiles
Before long
Her eyes will flutter open
And meet his gaze
But for now
He'll partake in his
Solitary bliss

we

I love that we don't
Have to work so hard
At this
That we don't spend our time
Trying to impress each other
Or be something
We're not
We can just spend time together
Whether curled up on the couch
Watching some dumb movie
Or having lunch at some no-name diner
I love that we can let our guard down
Around each other
And say whatever is on our minds
Not having to worry
About choosing our words
Or misunderstanding
Their meanings
I love that we have something
So simple
Yet so strong
So special
And I only see it getting better
As the days turn into weeks
The weeks turn into months
The months turn into years

got caught

You're not necessarily
Sorry you did it
You're just sorry
You got caught
And couldn't talk
Your way out of it
But you have no real remorse
For your actions
And the only thing you've learned
From it
It's how to better
Cover your tracks
Next time

see myself

I wish I could see myself
The way you see me
Instead of seeing
All of my flaws
Seeing the good in me
The beauty in me

space

Wanting my own space
Makes me feel
Selfish and anti-social
But at the same time
I need a place
That's mine
My own little sanctuary
Where I can go
Relax and recharge
And be ready to face the day

shades of gray

Normally
I like when things
Have that gray area
When there's options
And not a cut and dry
Yes or no answer
But this problem?
All there seems to be
Is gray
And no matter which way
I choose to look at it
I end up with
More questions
Than answers

one great idea

It's crunch time
And I feel like
I'm fighting
An uphill battle
To finish this thing
And prove people wrong
Even though
Nobody seems to really care
So instead of spending my nights
Getting an extra hour or two
Of sleep
I'm lying in bed
Typing away
And trying to
Make poetry
Out of nothing
Just hoping that
One great idea will
Pop into my head
And I can send my fingers
Flying furiously
Across the keyboard
But instead
All I get
Are these long
Drawn out
Drabbles
About nothing at all

one little moment

It was simple, really
Curled up in bed
Your arms around me
My back pressed against your chest
Your frame cradling mine
On a night no different
From all the rest
Save for one little moment
When you kissed my cheek
Took my hand
And slipped a ring
On my finger
And said
"I love you
And I want to keep
Loving you
Forever"

here's the thing

So, here's the thing
I like the attention
I've been getting from you
As of late
Even though
That's not the right way
To look at this
I like the way
You make me feel
No just on a
Sexual
Physical level
(Although that's really nice)
But the way you
Make me feel
About myself
Somewhere in the
Back of my mind
Is this little voice
Asking
'Could this be something more?'
'Could this be what should have been?'
But situations make it
Difficult
For me to get too involved
With you right now
So I sit back
And wait for your cue
And follow your lead
And see where it takes me
The fact that I'm even
Giving you as much thought
As I have been
Is a bit concerning

To be honest
But I also don't want
To close the door
On what could be a
Good opportunity
For me to be happy

I just wish I knew what to do
Wish I knew you
Just a little bit better
Then maybe we could actually
Have such a conversation
But I don't want to
Say the wrong thing
Or make assumptions
About where this might lead
For fear of
Chasing you off
Cuz I like the attention
And the way
You make me feel
Just a bit too much

concentrate

I find it's hard
To concentrate on anything
Particularly poetry
When the sounds of an
Industrial wood chipper
Are coming from next door
It jars me from my
Train of thought
And throws what little
Natural rhythm I've
Managed to find
Right off course
And by the time I find
My place again
That's about the time
They turn it back on

balance

Silently hoping I'll hear from you today
Makes me feel foolish
And needy
And desperate
But what little connection
We still seem to have
Makes me happy
So I walk that fine line
Between trying to show some interest
In you
And coming across too strong
Hoping I've got the
Balance right

clear night sky

Laying here under the light of the moon
Watching the twinkling stars
Dancing in the night sky
Snuggled close to keep warm
Falling under the spell of your touch
All through the night

Such a perfect night
Under the light of the moon
And the spell of your touch
I feel like I could reach the stars
As you hold me close and keep me warm
As I look up into the sky

And it's such a beautiful, clear sky
On an extraordinary night
The air is cool, but your body is warm
And your eyes sparkle in the light of the moon
Rivaling the stars
And I'm mesmerized by your simple touch

A gentle, caring touch
Under a dark, summer sky
And the twinkling stars
On a perfect night
Bathed in the soft light of the moon
Enjoying each other's warmth

You pull me close, keep me warm
Stroking my face with a gentle touch
And I'm over the moon
And as high as the sky
From such a perfect night
Under the twinkling stars

Under the twinkling stars
Snuggling close to stay warm
On this perfect summer night
Reveling in your sweet touch
Under a clear night sky
Washed in the soft glow of the moon

Bathed the light of a soft moon, looking up at the
twinkling stars
Under a summer night sky, keeping each other warm
I'm under the spell of your touch, and the blissfulness of
the night

first night

She stands before him
Baring her all
Save for a pair
Of pink panties
And he smiles
Hungrily
At her
Reaching for her
He pulls her close
His tongue darting out
To taste her sweetness
Dancing across her creamy white skin
She moves closer
Straddling his hips as she
Climbs onto his lap
Her arms around his neck
His lips at her collar bone
Along her neck
Teeth gently nipping at
Her earlobe
Her fingers tease their way
Along his neck
Down his back
As she tilts her head back
And lets her eyes close
Losing herself to the sensation
Slowly he lays back on the bed
Taking her with him
Their lips meet
Tongues tangling
His hands on her hips
Her hands slowly tangling in his hair
She teasingly makes her way
Down along his neck

His shoulders
His chest
Leaving a trail of kisses in her wake
Until she's at his stomach
She sits back up
Straddling his hips
And smiles down at him
Their eyes full of passion
And desire
On this,
Their first night together

simplest of kisses

I love how good you make me feel
With the simplest of kisses
And the gentlest of touches
Such passion
Such desire
Such wanting

You're all I want
With the way you make me feel
You're all I desire
I hunger for your kiss
Filled with such passion
And I long for your touch

Just one simple touch
Is all I want
Full of passion
It's all I need to feel
Just share with me one kiss
And show me your true desire

All I desire
Is your touch
And your kiss
It's all I could ever want
I love just how you make me feel
As you share with me your passion

So full of passion
And desire
And I long to feel
Your sensual touch
It's all I want
Just one more kiss

54

And oh, what a kiss
Exploding with passion
Echoing all I want
So full of desire
As I give in to your touch
Loving how it makes me feel

This is how I feel, as you pull me into your kiss
Your touch, so full of passion
You're all I desire, all I could ever want

safe side

I'm relieved
But cautious
About the good news
I got tonight
Just to be on the safe side
I'll probably double check again
In a few days
And make sure nothing has changed
But for now
It's a huge weight
Lifted off of my shoulders
And I can breathe
Even if just a little bit

never that simple

I light another cigarette
And pull up another empty page
Just hoping the words
Will somehow appear
Without really trying
But it's never that simple
Is it?
So I stare off
Into the distance
Searching for something
That might spark the creativity

turning 30

I'm practically days away
From turning thirty
And going through the myriad
Of feelings
That seem to go along with it
Like it's some magic number
Like things are going to change
Just because
I'm another year older
I thought the same thing at eighteen
At twenty-one
And twenty-five

usual worries

I love the evenings
Where my most prominent concern
Is which pair of shoes I should get
Or what color I should
Paint my nails
Not that there isn't
A number of other
More pressing things
I should be concerning myself with
At the moment
But that's what's on my mind
And it's a nice change of pace
From my usual worries

the volume

Someone please turn down the volume
For it's far too loud down in this hole
And the screams that slice
Like a hot knife through wax
Like the breaking of glass
Get me no closer to freedom

And my longing for freedom
Increases with the volume
As I pour another glass
Down here in this hole
The philosophical waning and waxing
Of the knife as it prepares its next slice

Could I interest you in a slice
Of a never-found freedom
That's been sealed over in an impenetrable wax
But seriously, check the volume
Before you climb down into this hole
And I'll gladly share what's in my glass

Yet another broken glass
Fingertips sliced
And I just want to feel whole
All I want is my freedom
And I lower my volume
As I succumb to the heat of the wax

My soul has been waxed
Until it sparkles like stained glass
And my silence speaks volumes
Shall I offer you a slice?
I'll trade it for a taste of freedom
If it'll get me out of this hole

What is the cost of feeling whole?
My morals wane and wax
As I ponder the cost of my freedom
And pour another glass
And take another slice
And your silence speaks volumes

Please turn down the volume, then join me in this hole
It's just a small slice, this unbalanced wane and wax
And we'll raise a glass, toasting this never-found
freedom

waiting

I want you
Need you
Next to me
On top of me
Inside me
Hands groping
Nails clawing
Teeth biting
I'm warm
And wet
And waiting
For you to
Devour me

learning a lot

I'm learning a lot
About myself lately
As I try and
Make sense
Of a decision made
Without thought

my enemy

You should be my enemy
After all,
You've done everything in your power
To undermine me
Undermine him
And undermine our relationship
But I can't bring myself to hate you
Not because of some
Moral issue with hate
But because I mostly
Feel sorry for you
Because you won't let him
Be happy while you're
So miserable
Because you took him for
Granted
And thought you could find
Someone better
And that you were stupid enough
To cast a really great guy aside
Because you were bored
For the little time I've
Know you
I've watched you make
One bad decision
After another
Whether you're just that clueless
Or you're self-sabotaging
I don't know
But I feel sorry for you
And wish I knew
How to help you
Move on and get over it

our plans

I can't help but smile
As I watch you
Pouring over my pile
Of wedding planning stuff
Flipping through magazines
Making notes on sticky paper
To leave on the pages for me
Most guys would,
I think,
Only be concerned with
What day and what time
But you?
This is your second chance
To make it right
The wedding
The marriage
And the happily ever after
But you make it so easy
To be with you
I can't imagine
This won't work
Forever
I watch you from the doorway
For a few more seconds
Before walking into the kitchen
Walking up behind you
And wrapping my arms around your neck
"I'm not screwing up your plans,
Am I?"
You ask as you turn and kiss my cheek
Before pulling me down into your lap
"Never,"
I reply
"And they're our plans, babe."

65

a chance

I'll do anything
To make it up to you
Just don't ask me
To leave
Just give me a chance
To explain
That what you think
You saw
Wasn't anything at all
I'd never
Do such a thing
Not to you
He's just a friend
Nothing more
Who's fighting for
His own relationship
Looking for advice
On his next move
So whatever it is
You think you saw
You're mistaken
Just give me a chance
To explain this to you
To make it up to you
Just don't ask me
To leave

spilled coffee

Spilled coffee
Stains the pages
Of my notebook
The only marks
On an
Otherwise blank page
That should be
Filled
With words linked
Together in some
Poetic form

going on

I can't believe
How much
I'm looking forward
To seeing you
In a month's time
I shouldn't be
Because what we've
Got going on
Is wrong on
So many levels

But oh,
How it feels so good

so easily

I can't believe
You can so easily
Talk me into
The things
You talk me into
It's so against
My nature
But a few sweet
And charming words
And I'm off
Granting your request

make this work

It's one more drink
One last cigarette
One more try
To make this work
If you only knew
How many
Last chances
You've had over the years
But I keep telling
Myself
"Maybe this time..."
Yet this time
Never seems to come around

stuck

I sit here and watch
As everyone else seems
To move on with their lives
Make something of themselves
While I'm stuck
In this loop
In this rut
I've spent too many years
Trying to figure out
How to take
That one step
That might lead me in a
Different direction
Only to find out
Too late
I should have taken a
Left
Instead of a
Right

longing

There's this longing
This need
This want
This desire
I can't quite describe
Can't quite figure out
But it's clear
That something's missing
And it's something
I crave

long neck

I watch her drink
And I don't think
She realizes
What she's doing to me
Her slender fingers
Wrapped around
The long-neck bottle
As she puts it to her
Full lips
And tilts it back
Letting her tongue linger
Along the edge
Just long enough
Even when she sets
The bottle down
On the bar
Her fingers slowly trail
Up and down
The sides
And it takes every once
Of my self-control
To not grab her by the arm
And whisk her away
To my truck
And back home
And into our bedroom

She catches me watching her
Out of the corner of her eye
And with a wink and a smile
She takes the long-neck between her lips
Slowly
Tilts the bottle back
And lets her tongue linger

73

At the edge
Just a little bit longer
Than before
Then runs it along
Her bottom lip
And I smile at her
Slowly shaking my head
Cuz it's clear she knows
Exactly what she's doing
To me
As she drinks her beer
From that long-neck bottle

call back

I feel bad
For not calling you back
Tonight
And plan to make
My apologies
In the morning

But...

There's also no reason
You couldn't have called
Me back
Instead

fate

I asked you
If you believed
In such things as
Fate
And love at
First sight
You were quiet
For a moment
Before pulling me closer
And telling me
"If fate was what
Brought me
To that particular bar
On the particular night,
Then yes.
And if there is such a thing
As love at
First sight
I didn't believe in it
Until I saw you."

poetry in the dark

There's something about
Writing poetry
In the dark
That just seems to make
The words flow
Onto the page
(Or in this case
The screen)
Maybe it's the absence of
Other distractions
Or the void of the
Darkness
Whatever it is
I'm taking advantage of it
For as long as I can

to myself

I like having my bed
All to myself
Sleeping right in the middle
Having the blanket
And all of the pillows
All to myself
If I thought you wouldn't
Take it personally
I'd suggest sleeping in
Separate beds
Every night

last ditch effort

It's a last minute dash
A last ditch effort
To try and get
Just one more poem
Written before midnight
Fingers crossed

look up

I like that when we
Lay in bed
You lay
Just a touch lower
Than me
You say it's because
It's one of the few times
You get to
Look up at me
And I laugh
And lean down
Just slightly
For a kiss

forgot about

There's nothing like feeling
Hopelessly behind
Grabbing your pen
And notebook
With the intention
Of writing furiously
To make up for lost time
And finding a few pages
Of poetry
Written a few weeks ago
That you forgot all about

counting down

Even though I try
To tell myself
Not to do it
I find myself
Counting down the days
Until I can see you again
I also find myself
Wishing you could come
To Buffalo with me
Trying to find a way
To spend my birthday with you
But I don't think
Either of those wishes
Are going to come true
So I settle for
Counting down the days
Until I can see you again
And make the most
Of what little time we'll have

go big

If you're gonna fuck up
Make sure you go big
And make it count

~~*~*~*

lost

I could spend hours
Getting lost in your eyes
Your smile

~~*~*~*

please everybody

I'm tired of fighting to please everybody
When clearly that's an impossible task
And something that never seems to be
Reciprocated

~~*~*~*

you are

You shouldn't be the one
That puts a smile on my face
That makes me feel this way
But you are

no idea

Sometimes I think
You have no idea
Just how much
In love with you
I am

~~*~*~*

competition

There's nothing wrong
With a little
Healthy competition
For my affection
Is there?

~~*~*~*

in my bed

I want you in my bed
Naked
And wanting
And willing

~~*~*~*

void

I feel like an empty void
Desperately trying to find
The one thing
That will satisfactorily
Fill the space

84

lucky

How did I get so lucky
To wake up next to
An angel in my bed
Every morning?

~~*~*~*

entangled

Our bodies entangled
Still covered in
A light sheen of sweat
Hearts still pounding

www.ingramcontent.com/pod-product-compliance
Lightning Source LLC
Chambersburg PA
CBHW031327040426
42443CB00005B/242